IMAGES
of America

THE BUILDING OF THE
OROVILLE DAM

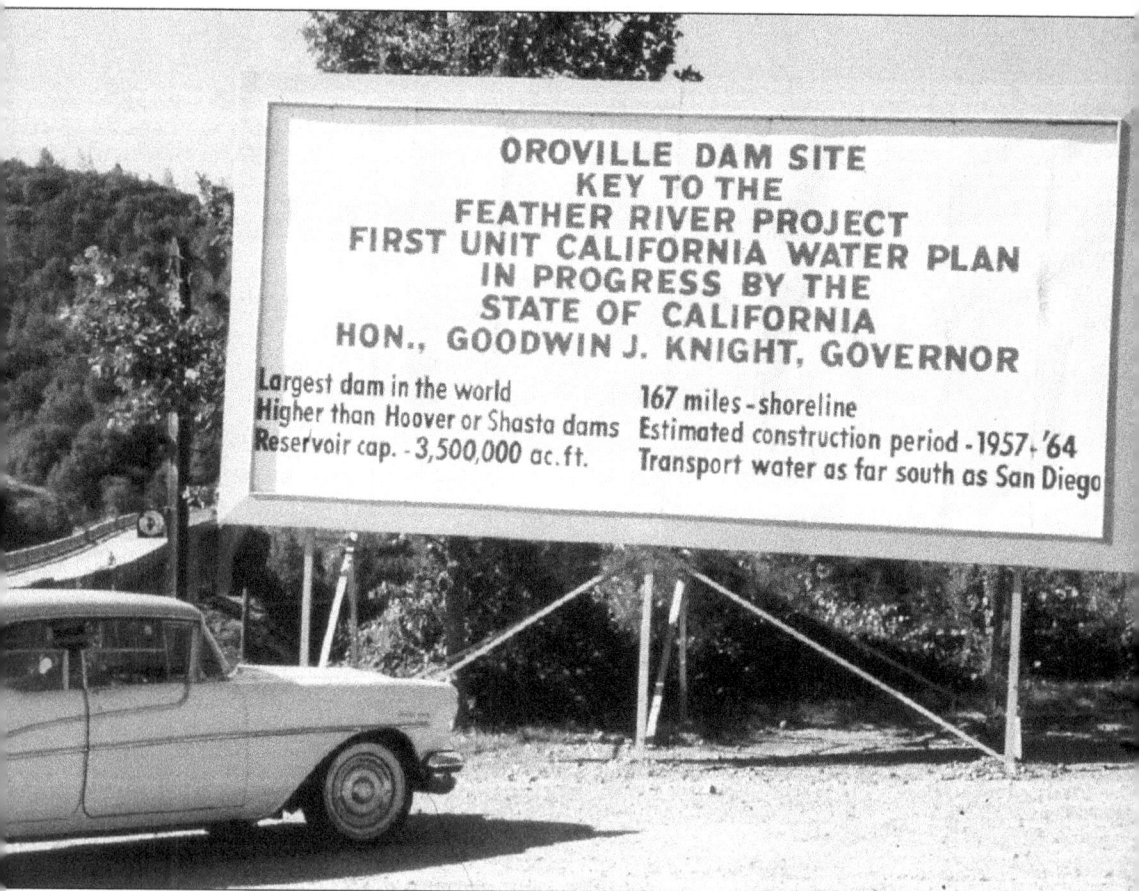

This photograph from 1957 shows the very first billboard to be erected at the Oroville Dam site. It was put up shortly after Gov. Goodwin Knight designated the area as the site of the pending Oroville Dam. The information on the billboard was modified when Gov. Edmund G. Brown took office in 1959. Construction of the dam was completed in 1968. (Courtesy of Butte County Historical Society.)

ON THE COVER: Engine No. 8010 is seen in good times in late 1963. It is at the borrow area, taking on material. An unlucky engine, it was involved in a fatal accident at the borrow on April 9, 1964, when it collided with a Cat 660 scraper. It also was totally destroyed in a head-on collision on October 7, 1965, in which four crewmen were killed. (Courtesy of Butte County Historical Society.)

IMAGES
of America

THE BUILDING OF THE
OROVILLE DAM

Larry R. Matthews

ARCADIA
PUBLISHING

Published by Arcadia Publishing
Charleston, South Carolina

Library of Congress Control Number: 2013938692

For all general information, please contact Arcadia Publishing:
Telephone 843-853-2070
Fax 843-853-0044
E-mail sales@arcadiapublishing.com
For customer service and orders:
Toll-Free 1-888-313-2665

Visit us on the Internet at www.arcadiapublishing.com

This book is dedicated to the 34 construction workers who died
working on the various projects related to the Oroville Dam.

CONTENTS

ACKNOWLEDGMENTS

The various agencies and individuals listed here provided assistance and authorized the use of their photographs for this project. My thanks go out to Nancy Brower, Lucy Sperlin, Sally McCoy, and Bill Burg of the Butte County Historical Society (BCHS). Thanks also to Michael J. Miller and Paul Hames of the Graphic Services Branch of the California Department of Water Resources (CDWR). Charlie and Judy Jensen (CJ) of Oroville contributed photographs that Charlie took in the first few days after the train tunnel disaster. Gene Merian (GM) of Oroville; Michael Hogan (MH) of Oroville; Janet Dawson (JD) of Paradise; Jerry Topper of Roseville; Gene Topper (GT) of Tucson, Arizona; and Jim McDonnell and the South Oroville African American Historical Society (SOAAHS) contributed multiple photographs from their collections. Contributing single photographs were Marvin McTigue of Fullerton, Albert M. King Sr. and Jr., and Garrett Jackson, all of Oroville. Tony Ciaffoni of Brisbane, Australia, provided a successful lead regarding a very unique Bidwell Bar photograph. Image sources in this book are identified either by name or by the abbreviations included here.

My thanks go to Jerry Topper for the information about his father, Gene Topper, and their dog Moose. I am grateful to Gene for sharing his unique and charming story and photographs.

Special thanks to Scott Roberts of Yuba City, who provided me with technical assistance and some photographs and who accompanied me in finding long-lost Oroville Dam–related historical locations.

I would also like to thank my wife, Sharon; my family; and all of those friends in Butte, Sutter, and Yuba Counties who were so supportive of this project. We all reside downriver from the Oroville Dam and know how truly valuable it is to our area.

I want to thank the memory and talent of the late Butte County historical writer Bill Talbitzer. Bill's many books about Oroville-area history first fascinated me in 1963 and have continued to inspire my writing.

Researching for this project could have been tedious. Instead, those mentioned above helped make it a joy. They will always have my thanks.

INTRODUCTION

The small mining town of Ophir was established in October 1850 in California's northern Sacramento Valley. It was founded along the Feather River where it flows out of the Sierra Nevada Mountains and turns south.

Millions of dollars in gold and some diamonds were found in the area. Some miners struck it rich, but many went broke. By 1856, the town was renamed Oroville (based upon the Spanish word for "gold" and the French word for "town").

At one time, Oroville was the largest mining town and the fifth-largest town in California. In addition to the mining industry, Oroville was essentially an agricultural community, and very successful nut and fruit industries continue to flourish there even today.

In 1906, the city of Oroville was incorporated. It had previously become the county seat of Butte County in 1856 after the cities of Hamilton and Bidwell Bar had held the honor for a short time.

From 1898 to 1918, enormous gold dredges plied the Feather River area. It is estimated that $30 million in gold was recovered in the Oroville area. The use of dredges left acres and acres of ponds and enormous piles of rock. Those rock piles would play an integral part in what was to come later. By 1950, the state of California was concerned about water. Sometimes, there was too much, but mostly there was too little, especially in Southern California.

There had been major floods on the Feather River in 1906, 1907, 1909, 1928, 1937, and 1955. These disasters had greatly affected Oroville and the Marysville–Yuba City area that is located 30 miles south.

In 1957, preliminary work had started on the plan to build the Oroville Dam, a major part of the California State Water Project. The dam location would be nine miles to the northeast of Oroville, near the confluence of the North, Middle, and South Forks of the Feather River. At 770 feet, it would be the highest earth-filled dam in the world—44 feet higher than Hoover Dam. It was estimated that the dam would impound more than three and a half million acre-feet of water and that the lake would have a shoreline of 167 miles. Much of the dam would be constructed with many of those supposedly useless rocks left over from the old gold-dredging operations.

But there was much more to the project than just the big dam, and this book will attempt to document that fact. For miles around, the area would be transformed. There were canals, bridges, roads, dams, tunnels, and railroads to be built or rerouted. All of the trees had to be removed from the proposed lake area. Two enormous powerhouses needed to be built: one beneath the dam and the other at the Thermalito Power House. A forebay and afterbay also needed to be constructed.

There was history to be saved or destroyed. In the lake area, 350 pioneer graves needed to be excavated and relocated. The town of Bidwell Bar had to be burned down, the old Enterprise Bridge needed to be demolished, and Hansell's Bridge had to be blown up. The historic 1856 Bidwell Bar Bridge, tollhouse, and Mother Orange Tree all had to be removed and relocated.

Some history would be lost. Holes would be gouged out of McLaughlin's Wall, and it would be inundated by the waters behind the Thermalito Diversion Dam.

There was also a whole new railroad to build. The Oro Dam Constructors Railroad moved all of the rock materials, and the length of the route was 12 miles. It started at the borrow area, located on the west side of the Feather River southwest of Oroville. It then crossed to the east side of the river, traveled north, and crossed to the north side of the river. From there, it went east, traveling under the Highway 70 freeway bridge and recrossing the river between the Upper Thermalito Bridge and the new fish hatchery dam. Traveling along the east side of the river, it ran north and east, through an old railroad tunnel, and then on to the construction site of the dam. This material-handling system was one of the very first to be designed by computer.

During construction, 34 workers died. Four perished at that old railroad tunnel in a tragedy that is documented in this book. Others were killed by explosions, vehicle collisions, electrocutions, falls, strokes, and heart attacks.

Mother nature did not always cooperate with the construction. In 1962, 1963, and 1964, major flooding ravaged the construction sites of the main dam, the Thermalito Diversion Dam, and the fish hatchery dam. It can be supposed that this was nature's way of illustrating one of the reasons why the project was necessary.

This enormous project brought in construction crews from all over the world. Some brought their families, and some came alone. Some stayed a few months or a year before moving on to the next construction project, and some who came to work on the dam in 1961 still live in the Oroville area.

Gov. Edmund G. Brown signaled the beginning of major construction in 1961 with a dynamite blast, and Gov. Ronald Reagan came for the dedication of the dam in 1968. That seven-year period was a hectic, thrilling, and rewarding time of activity for the citizens of the area.

Since its completion, the Oroville Dam has provided much-needed water, power, recreational facilities, and flood control. That flood control has, most probably, saved many lives. It certainly made later floods—in February 1986 and January 1997—less destructive.

On June 1, 1957, California governor Goodwin Knight visited the proposed dam site. A jerky color film of his visit survives. In that seven-minute silent film, he can be seen speaking from the caboose of his train at the dam site. Also shown are Hansell's Bridge and the wide white line that was drawn on the hillside to show where the edge of the dam would be. The film captures a parade in downtown Oroville and a barbecue at Hewitt Park in celebration of the proposed dam. That was the beginning of the project.

This book attempts to show the building of the dam and most of its other ancillary projects and illustrate just what a superhuman effort it took to create. I also hope to help document some of the history that was lost and show how much history was saved.

To this day, I believe that the citizens of the Oroville area and the surviving construction workers are justifiably proud of this "Colossus on the Feather River."

One

BEFORE THE DAM

This very early view of Ophir from 1854 looks up Myers Street toward the north. In 1856, the town was renamed Oroville and was designated as the county seat. (Courtesy of BCHS.)

This is one of the enormous gold dredges that plied the Feather River from 1898 to 1918. In the Oroville area, $30 million in gold was gleaned from the river. What they left behind was an eyesore—thousands of acres of rocks and ponds. This photograph was taken in the early 1900s by John Hogan. (Courtesy of CDWR.)

Here is a late-1950s view of some of the 6,000 acres of dredge tailings that had been considered a blight on the landscape for more than half a century. These turned out to be a gold mine in themselves once it was realized that they were a perfect commodity to use in the construction of Oroville Dam. (Courtesy of JD.)

These aerial photographs from the late 1950s show the future Oroville Dam site. Hansell's Bridge can be seen crossing the Middle Fork of the Feather River. Highway 24, the original route through Oroville to the Feather River Canyon and on to Reno, Nevada, crosses the bridge. Because of the construction of the dam at this location, Highway 70 was completed in 1962 to replace this route. The photograph above shows Bald Rock near the upper right-hand corner. In the photograph at right is a clearer view of the Western Pacific Rail line that ran through the area and to points east. (Above, courtesy of CDWR; right, courtesy of BCHS.)

Bidwell Bar, seen here in 1854, was located near the junction of the North and Middle Forks of the Feather River, 11 miles northeast of Oroville. John Bidwell found gold at this site in 1848 and established the settlement. By 1854, it had a post office, a newspaper, and a population of more than 3,000. (Courtesy of BCHS.)

This late-19th-century photograph shows a horse and buggy crossing Bidwell Bar Bridge. Also shown are the tollhouse on the left and the Mother Orange Tree on the right. The tree was planted at Bidwell Bar in 1856 by Judge Joseph Lewis. It was called the Mother Orange Tree because so many seedling trees were started from it. (Courtesy of BCHS.)

An example of why Oroville Dam was needed for flood control was a series of major storms that occurred from December 1906 to March 1907. One of the most massive storms to damage the Oroville area flooded the town. The picture above was taken by a photographer standing on Bird Street, looking north up Myers Street toward the Feather River. The image below shows six Oroville residents in front of Mason's Laundry, taking in the flood in a surprisingly casual way. As a result of this flood, the town soon built levees and further reinforced them in the 1930s. (Above, courtesy of MH; below, courtesy of BCHS.)

The flood in March 1907 wrecked the Feather River Bridge and completely washed away the center span. The image above shows the west side of the bridge at low water level. At left is a view toward the north. A replacement iron bridge, built between 1907 and 1910, served until the 1980s, when a concrete road bridge was constructed just upstream from it. The 1907 Upper Thermalito Bridge still stands as a historic relic and serves as a way across the Feather River for pedestrians and bicyclists. (Above, courtesy of MH; left, courtesy of BCHS.)

These are photographs of the Bidwell Bar area. In the 1880s image above, the Hess-Larcombe Store can be seen in the middle, and the Bendle Store stands to the left. The photograph below, from the 1920s, shows some vintage automobiles near the building in the right corner. On the left is the old 1856 bridge. The Gold Rush times had been wild, with prospectors even digging holes in the streets and under the foundations of buildings to gain access to the gold. The town had offered theatrical performances, dances, a bookstore, and quite a few bars, and for a time, it had been the county seat of Butte County. By the time the photograph below was taken, Bidwell Bar was just a sleepy little village of about 40 people. The days of wealth had lasted a very short time—from 1848 until the gold had been virtually exhausted in 1856. (Both, courtesy of BCHS.)

These photographs show John Bendle's store at Bidwell Bar in 1960. The structure was more than 110 years old when the site was covered by the waters of Lake Oroville. The formidable rock building served as a store for many years and, in at least one instance, served temporarily as a jail. On the night of June 4, 1871, George Sharkovich was captured at the Bidwell Bar Bridge after murdering young Susie McDaniel of Cherokee. Bridge keeper Isaac Ketchum and a guard by the name of McBride took him to the store for temporary confinement. When he went for a weapon and attempted to escape, John Bendle shot him dead. The building, originally known as the Gluckauf Store, was one of the last remaining structures of Bidwell Bar. It was demolished just prior to being inundated by Lake Oroville. (Both, courtesy of BCHS.)

This view shows just how popular the Curry-Bidwell Bar Recreation Area was as a swimming and picnicking destination prior to the building of the Oroville Dam. This photograph from July 4, 1960, shows children and adults enjoying the eastern bank of the Feather River. A lifeguard is on duty to alleviate any danger. (Courtesy of BCHS.)

This photograph shows children sitting on a diving board as swimmers enjoy the cool water and beach on the western bank of the Feather River during a hot summer day prior to 1963. The historic Bidwell Bar Bridge served as a footbridge, diving platform, and also as a reminder of the area's rich Gold Rush history. (Courtesy of Albert M. King Sr. and Jr.)

Jodi Jackson and her brother Garrett sit on a rock and enjoy the cool waters of the Feather River at Bidwell Bar on a hot August day in 1960. Garrett states he was five years old here, his sister, six. They lived in Feather Falls Village and came down the hill to Bidwell Bar several times a week to cool off. Their father, Bob Jackson, was principal at Feather Falls School. (Courtesy of Garrett Jackson.)

This is the Bidwell Bar Cemetery in the late 1950s. There were various other private cemeteries nearby. Hundreds of residents had been buried in the Bidwell Bar and Enterprise areas since 1848, and prior to the inundation of the area, more than 300 were removed from the canyon and reinterred in the area of Thompson Flat. (Courtesy of BCHS.)

These views show the simple beauty of the old bridge at Bidwell Bar in the late 1950s. In the 1850s, there was high water during the winter, and a ferry was insufficient to carry parties across the Feather River. Therefore, in 1853, the residents of Bidwell Bar raised funds for a bridge. The structure was manufactured by Starbucks Iron Works in Troy, New York, and was transported by clipper ship around the "horn" of South America to San Francisco. From there, it was barged upriver to Marysville and then brought by team and wagon to Bidwell Bar. The bridge was opened in 1856 and remained in use until automobile traffic was banned because of structural issues in 1954. It is the first suspension bridge west of the Mississippi River. (Both, courtesy of BCHS.)

One of the largest and oldest buildings in Bidwell Bar was the two-story Bidwell Bar Store. It offered "eats [and] drinks" and a Flying A gas station. It had been around for 116 years when it came to its end on November 20, 1964. The inundation of the area by Lake Oroville was pending, and it had been decided that it was much more efficient to burn down Bidwell Bar than to tear it down and haul it off. Therefore, on that day, all wooden buildings in the Bidwell Bar area were burned, as seen below. Lucky Lager, Hamms, and Burgie Beer neon signs remain in the front windows of the burning building as a reminder of Bidwell Bar's wilder times. (Both, courtesy of BCHS.)

Here are two more views of the burning of the Bidwell Bar Store. The local media described November 20, 1964, as the day Bidwell Bar "ceased to exist as a town." The burning commenced at 8:00 a.m. and included the town's water tower, store, tavern, homes, and junk piles. More than one hundred years of history went up in flames. The town had been, for a short time, the Butte County seat of government beginning in 1853. It had been the site of the county's first newspaper and school district, and it was also the site of the first gold-fluming operation on the Feather River. Only a few stone structures were left to face the rising waters. (Both, courtesy of BCHS.)

This is the rail junction of Bidwell that lay one mile west of Bidwell Bar. It too was put to the torch on November 20, 1964, as part of the clean-up operation in Bidwell Canyon. Here, two California Department of Water Resources employees make their way down the tracks after setting fire to a shack. Their 1959 International Travelall awaits their return. (Courtesy of BCHS.)

This 1962 photograph is of the Enterprise Bridge that crossed the South Fork of the Feather River. Enterprise was located about five miles east of Bidwell Bar. Prior to the inundation of the area by Lake Oroville, this bridge was removed and scrapped. A new Enterprise Bridge was built hundreds of feet higher on Lumpkin Road to facilitate access to the Feather Falls area. (Courtesy of BCHS.)

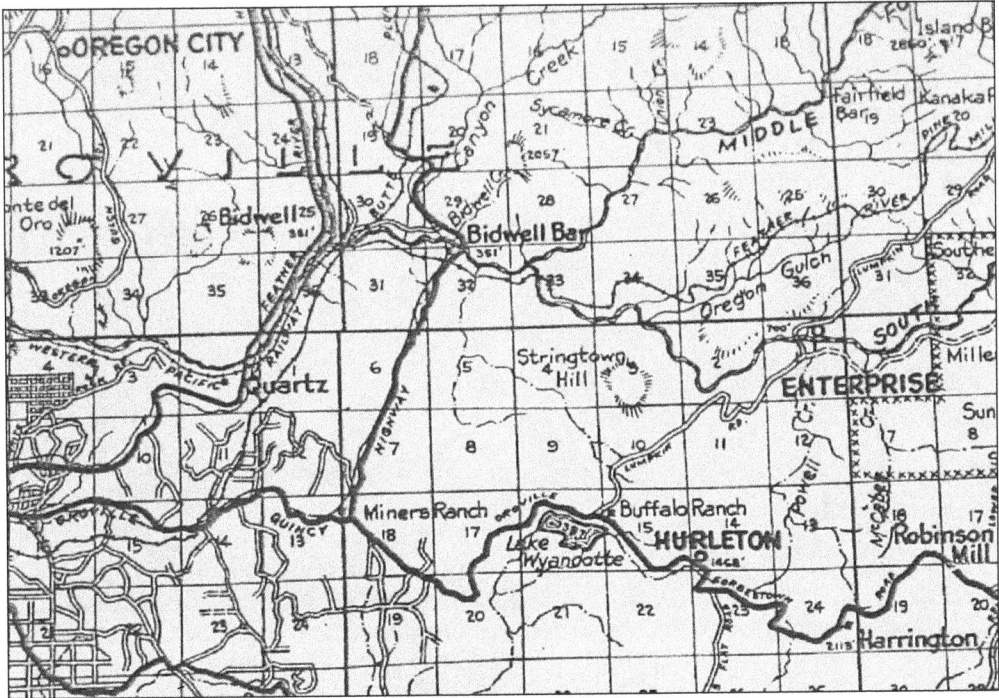

This old map from 1930 shows the canyon area that was flooded by Lake Oroville. The communities of Bidwell, Bidwell Bar, and Enterprise are identified. The future location of Oroville Dam is right above where the word "Quartz" is shown. (Courtesy of BCHS.)

Maj. Frank McLaughlin's Wall is shown in 1963. It was part of a failed gold-mining venture to divert the Feather River and was built between 1894 and 1896. It ran for two miles along the Feather River. The operation was the first such project to be illuminated by electric light, and the lights were provided by Thomas A. Edison. (Author's photograph.)

This late-1896 photograph of Maj. Frank McLaughlin's mining operation, the Golden Feather, shows the venture in full operation. The cost had been $12 million, and the operation failed. McLaughlin's British financial backers took a great loss, but he personally came out ahead on the deal. On November 1, 1897, the major blew up the dam and flume with 1,000 pounds of dynamite. While in his mansion in Santa Cruz on November 17, 1907, exactly two years after his wife died, the major shot his daughter and took poison. (Courtesy of BCHS.)

McLaughlin's Wall is visited in 1964 by Joseph Lenderskis. For him and many others, the area was a popular place for hiking. Lenderskis owned JL Automotive Service from 1963 until 1979. (Author's photograph.)

In the fall of 1964, bulldozers gouged out holes in McLaughlin's Wall to facilitate flooding of the area and left no portion for posterity. The wall was also commonly referred to as the "Chinese Wall" as Chinese workers had helped build it. (Courtesy of BCHS.)

This image from November 1964 shows the beginning of the inundation of McLaughlin's Wall by the waters formed by the Thermalito Diversion Dam. The wall lies in its watery grave near the old Oro Dam Railway train tunnel. (Author's photograph.)

This March 1962 northwesterly view shows the intersection of Oro Dam Boulevard and Washington Avenue in the lower center. The Central Lanes Bowling Alley is in the northeast corner of the intersection. Oroville High School's Bechtol Field and the Feather Plunge Pool can be seen in the middle right of the photograph. A brand-new Montgomery Ward and Safeway store would occupy the bare ground on the left side of Washington Avenue within a few years. The proposed dam was bringing in new building projects along with more residents. The residents were very excited about what the next years would bring. (Courtesy of BCHS.)

Two

Ceremony and Construction

On July 5, 1956, California governor Goodwin Knight signed the bill that combined several California agencies into the California Department of Water Resources. He then directed that department to form a plan to establish the State Water Project. On June 1, 1957, he visited the future site of Oroville Dam by train and also traveled to Oroville to celebrate its selection as the site of the dam. Knight served as governor from 1953 to 1959. He lived to see the completion of Oroville Dam, passing away on May 22, 1970. (Courtesy of MH.)

WESTERN PACIFIC
R.R. RELOCATION
MAY 29, 1962

THERMALITO
POWER CANAL

CHEROKEE
ROAD
BRIDGE

THERMALITO
AFTERBAY

NELSON AVE.
BRIDGE

THERMALITO
POWER PLANT

CHICO
ROAD BRIDGE

WESTERN CANAL AND
RICHVALE CANAL OUTLETS

FISH BARRIER DAM
FEATHER RIVER
FISH HATCHERY

THERMALITO
FOREBAY DAM

ROUTE
162
BRIDGE

LARKIN ROAD BRIDGE

THERMALITO AFTERBAY

OROVILLE-WILLOWS
ROAD RELOCATION

RIVER OUTLETS

THERMALITO
AFTERBAY

28

This California Department of Water Resources map from July 1965 shows the relationship between the Oroville Dam and various other projects. The Middle Fork (new Bidwell Bar) Bridge's location is on the far right. The towns of Bidwell Bar and Enterprise are located just west of the bridge, now at the bottom of Lake Oroville. To the west is the Oroville Dam and Power Plant. Just a bit north of Oroville's location are the Thermalito Dam, the fish hatchery dam, and the Thermalito Diversion Canal. The location of the Dam Train Tunnel wreck is where the Feather River makes a 90-degree turn to the east. To the west of Oroville are the Thermalito Forebay and Thermalito Power Plant. A bit more to the southwest is the Thermalito Afterbay. (Courtesy of CDWR.)

As its existing Western Pacific Railroad route would be inundated by Lake Oroville, one of the first things to be accomplished was the rerouting of the Western Pacific Railroad. This photograph from July 28, 1959, shows the building of the line's rail bridge across the Feather River about a mile north of Oroville. The new railroad would cross this bridge and be routed around the west side of Table Mountain before crossing the lake on West Branch Bridge. (Courtesy of MH.)

These construction workers measure the amount of fill material in a specific area of the borrow pit. Once determined, the amount of fill would then be removed either by draglines or by the enormous bucket-wheel excavators. The fill would then be trucked to conveyor belts. This photograph was taken on May 31, 1960. (Courtesy of CDWR.)

This photograph from May 8, 1961, is of the construction of the West Branch Bridge, a double-deck structure with a road bridge on top and a railroad bridge running beneath. This view looks southwest toward Wick's Corner on Highway 40 (later renamed Highway 70). The old West Branch Bridge can be seen on the left. The West Branch of Lake Oroville now flows beneath this bridge, which is 2,731 feet long and 450 feet high. (Courtesy of CDWR.)

Looking north, here is a close-up view of the construction of the West Branch Bridge in 1961. The bridge was the scene of one of the fatal accidents on the Oroville Dam project. On September 22, 1961, a painter fell from it. This bridge handles Highway 70 traffic from the Sacramento Valley to Plumas County and points east. (Courtesy of BCHS.)

This photograph captures the moment that Gov. Edmund G. Brown pushed the button to set off the first blast for the first diversion tunnel at the Oroville Dam on October 12, 1961. This marked the beginning of the construction of the project. From this spot, the tunnel was driven more than 4,400 feet into the hillside. (Courtesy of CDWR.)

The ground-breaking ceremony and opening dynamite blast on October 12, 1961, brought out a large crowd. Included in that crowd were television, radio, and newspaper organizations; local politicians; and the local high school band, drill team, and majorettes. Representatives from local Air Force bases included air police and Wafs who provided security. (Courtesy of CDWR.)

These two photographs were taken at the ground-breaking of the Oroville Dam on October 12, 1961. At right, Gov. Edmund G. "Pat" Brown poses with his finger on the button of the detonator box that will send the electrical charge to set off the first dynamite explosion. Below, the governor is shown with California Department of Water Resources director William E. Warne and some of the visitors who attended the ceremony that day. Governor Brown was a major advocate for the Oroville Dam and the California State Water Project. For a time, there was a movement to name the lake after him. However, the idea of calling the lake "Lake Brown" did not prove popular. Brown served as governor from January 5, 1959, to January 2, 1967, and passed away on February 16, 1996. (Both, courtesy of CDWR.)

Posing in front of the Prospector's Village sign are some of the managers for Oro Dam Constructors. They are, from left to right, Bruce Ferrell, Whit Little, John Fowler, Walter Siegel, Bob Fowler, Claude Johnston, and Charles Denham. Located on Oro Dam Boulevard, Prospector's Village was a popular dining and entertainment establishment for decades. A Holiday Inn Express and Sonic Drive-In now occupy that site. (Courtesy of CDWR.)

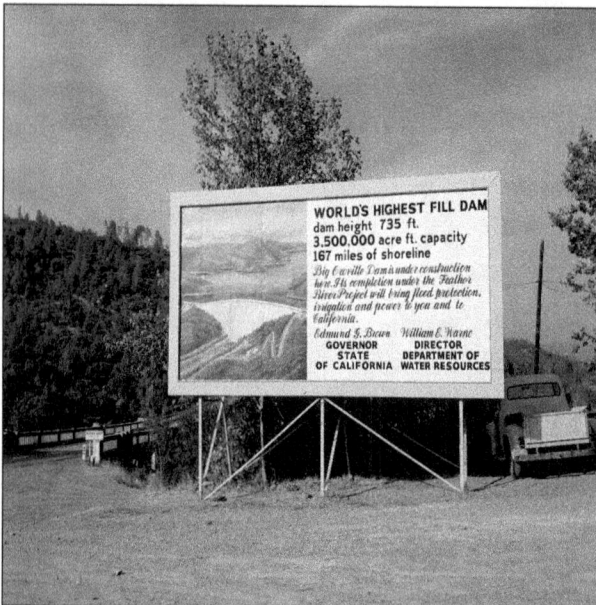

The billboard that stood at the dam site is pictured on October 12, 1961. The approach to the old Hansell's Bridge is to the left. Interestingly, the dam would be even higher than the billboard advertised. Its final height of 770 feet made it 44 feet higher than the Hoover Dam. (Courtesy of CDWR.)

This photograph was taken looking east from the southern approach of the Upper Thermalito Bridge. It shows the damage on the Feather River at the point where the Oroville fish hatchery dam is located. The hatchery dam had been partially completed but was then damaged by the high storm flows in October 1962. (Courtesy of CDWR.)

This aerial view from October 14, 1962, shows flood damage to the Feather River Fish Hatchery area and hatchery dam. Downstream and toward the southeast is the Upper Thermalito Bridge. On the left side of the bridge is Bridge Street, which becomes Table Mountain Boulevard once the bridge is crossed. The railroad on the left side is the Western Pacific Railroad. (Courtesy of CDWR.)

This view looks west and shows the dam site on October 14, 1962. In the middle is Hansell's Bridge. Work on the very first visitor's overlook, that wide area in the middle of the photograph, is in progress. The cleared area nearest to the camera is the beginning of the second visitor overlook, which would not be needed until the dam rose several hundred feet higher. (Courtesy of CDWR.)

This photograph of the flooded site of Diversion Tunnel No. 1 was taken two days after the October 12, 1962 Columbus Day storm that caused damage to the dam site and the fish hatchery dam. A damaged Bailey drawbridge can be seen. Frazier-Davis Construction Company lost several hundred thousand dollars in equipment in this storm, which dumped 3.77 inches of rain on the Oroville area. It also dumped seven inches of rain on the San Francisco Bay area. (Courtesy of CDWR.)

This view shows the remains of the original Bailey bridge lying in the Feather River. The structure was destroyed by the October 1962 floods, a loss of $75,000. It was replaced by a new Bailey bridge, which was later damaged in another storm in January 1963 when the water level rose 50 feet in 48 hours. (Courtesy of BCHS.)

This photograph shows the damage done in the area of the Feather River Fish Hatchery dam after the water level has receded from the flood of October 1962. As can be seen, all of the coffer cells have been destroyed, and there is a collapsed 30-ton crane stranded in the middle of the Feather River. (Courtesy of BCHS.)

Blasting for Diversion Tunnel No. 2 on January 12, 1963, took place at the base of Hansell's Bridge. Both Diversion Tunnel Nos. 1 and 2 would be 35 feet in diameter and would be used to divert the Feather River around the construction site. Both tunnels were driven into the mountain to a length of more than 4,400 feet. (Courtesy of CDWR.)

By January 12, 1963, Diversion Tunnel No. 1 had fully recovered from its October 1962 flood. In the foreground, a Caterpillar 46A bulldozer "Cat" pushes dirt so that a diesel shovel can load it into dump trucks. The dirt was being removed from an area so that the Hyatt Powerhouse could be built. Near the end of January 1963, another storm caused damage at the dam site. (Courtesy of CDWR.)

This is a view of the tunnel contractor's damaged Bailey bridge after the January 1963 storms. The bridge has been knocked off its hinge by floating debris. Afterward, the bridge was reinforced with timber cribbing to help it withstand future floods. (Courtesy of CDWR.)

On April 24, 1963, Gov. Edmund G. Brown returned to the dam site. With him was William E. Warne, director of the California Department of Water Resources. The event was the first concrete pour for the dam. Intermixed into the first pour was sand and gravel from all 58 California counties. (Courtesy of CDWR.)

Construction workers mix sand and gravel from all 58 California counties and funnel it into a Euclid R24 dump truck. Euclid produced heavy construction trucks, ranging from 10- to 62-ton capacity, from 1924 until the company was sold to Japan's Hitachi Construction company in 1993. Construction workers called these trucks "Eucs." This photograph was taken on April 24, 1963. (Courtesy of CDWR.)

April 24, 1963, is considered to be the formal beginning of the actual construction of Oroville Dam as it was the day that the first bucket of concrete was poured. In the background can be seen Gov. Edmund G. Brown. The bucket is being controlled by William E. Warne, director of the California Department of Water Resources. (Courtesy of CDWR.)

This April 29, 1963, photograph shows a crew washing and cleaning the dam site's core block area, which had to be cleaned down to the bedrock prior to any concrete pouring. The amount of concrete poured into the core block was 231,000 cubic yards. The core block acted as a toe for the embankment that would be placed during the 1964 season. (Courtesy of CDWR.)

This view of the dam site, looking southwest, shows the very beginnings of core block construction. Most methods used to construct the core block were the same as those used on Hoover Dam. Concrete was cooled prior to placement, was delivered by cableway, and was placed in a series of blocks of varying elevations. This photograph was taken on July 3, 1963. (Courtesy of CDWR.)

The aerial photograph at left, taken on July 3, 1963, looks south and shows that work has progressed on the Oroville fish hatchery dam since the floods of the previous October and January. Workmen have placed new coffer cells on the east side of the river to facilitate concrete pour. Later, the fish hatchery itself would be built on the west side of the river. Below is a close-up of the same scene from the east side of the river. (Left, courtesy of CDWR; below, courtesy of BCHS.)

This close-up image of the core block shows the overhead cableway used for the delivery of concrete. The cable had a 1,400-foot span and could unload an eight-cubic-yard bucket. It was the same cableway that was used for handling the powerhouse concrete for Glen Canyon Dam in Arizona. This photograph was taken on July 3, 1963, looking east. (Courtesy of CDWR.)

This August 19, 1963, aerial view looking north shows the northern end of the Oro Dam Railway. The fill trains traveled along the east edge of the Feather River and went through a tunnel just prior to the point where the Feather River turns east. After leaving the tunnel, they continued east toward the dam site. This tunnel is the site of the fatal train collision of October 7, 1965. (Courtesy of CDWR.)

Located on the west side of the Feather River, this is the eastern end of the train-loading station. It was still under construction at the time of this August 30, 1963, photograph. When in operation, rock virtually buried this machine, and empty trains ran through its middle and were filled with rock, or "cobbles," as it was normally called. (Courtesy of CDWR.)

This is the No. 1 Rail Haul Bridge that was located just a short distance to the east of the borrow area. Full Oro Dam Railroad trains would cross this bridge to the eastern shore of the Feather River and turn north. The borrow area is located just a few miles southwest of downtown Oroville. This photograph was taken on August 30, 1963. (Courtesy of CDWR.)

This is another view of the No. 1 Rail Haul Bridge, looking west. In the background is the train-loading station. When this photograph was taken on August 30, 1963, rails were being laid. Over the next four years, twin 2,500-horsepower diesel-electric locomotives, operating as a single-power unit, made more than 41,000 round trips across this bridge. (Courtesy of CDWR.)

This train is stopped at the point where the railroad crosses the Feather River just west of the Highway 70 freeway overpass. This photograph, taken on August 30, 1963, looks north. The train, continuing on south, found its way back to the borrow area. The Oro Dam Railroad, with its new engines, went into full operation on October 1, 1963. (Courtesy of CDWR.)

This photograph from August 30, 1963, shows track being laid on Rail Haul Bridge No. 3. The bridge was located right between the Upper Thermalito Bridge and the fish hatchery dam. Crews were putting on the finishing touches to the railroad as fill trains would begin regular service only a month later. (Courtesy of CDWR.)

This view looking northeast shows more progress on the fish hatchery dam. This time, construction crews placed new coffer cells on the north side of the river. Concrete was now readied for placement in that area. Monte de Oro appears in the background. This photograph was taken on August 30, 1963. (Courtesy of CDWR.)

The dam site is seen here on August 30, 1963. This is the eight-foot-wide conveyor system that brought rock from the car-dumping station across the river to the sorting area. The rock would then be stockpiled. The conveyor carried material at the maximum rate of 12,000 tons per hour. (Courtesy of CDWR.)

These are the Croil-Reynolds aggregate-cooling–system towers that were located at the dam site. They were previously used at the Keystone Dam in Oklahoma. The aggregate is cooled while stored in the five vacuum tanks. Three are for coarse material and two for sand. This photograph was taken on August 30, 1963. (Courtesy of CDWR.)

Crews assist in placing concrete at the core block in this photograph taken on August 30, 1963. The towers that supported the cableway were mounted on tracks and were able to move 400 feet. Two diesel locomotives shuttled between the batch plant and the loading dock, each pulling an eight-cubic-yard hopper car that discharged into the bucket fixed to the cableway. (Courtesy of CDWR.)

This is the scene at the dam site on October 1, 1963, the Oro Oro Dam Railway's first official day of operation. Engine No. 8012 and its trailing engine have eased under the Wellman dumper for a test run of the route and dump operation. (Courtesy of CDWR.)

Here, gunite being mixed in the right foreground is being applied by the two workmen on the support at left. Gunite has been in wide use in construction since 1914. Once application was completed, the Feather River was diverted down this new channel so it could flow around the core block. This photograph was taken on August 30, 1963. (Courtesy of CDWR.)

This is a close-up view of two workmen applying gunite to the west side of the new core block diversion canal on August 30, 1963. Gunite is a mixture of cement, sand, and water. Using a cement gun, dry material is blown out of the hose by compressed air, and water is injected at the nozzle as it is released. (Courtesy of CDWR.)

The photograph above from early 1963 shows the ongoing work in Diversion Tunnel No. 1. The photograph at left, from August 30, 1963, shows the finished inside. This tunnel, at 4,418 feet in length, is the shorter of the two. Tunnel No. 2 is 4,589 feet in length. Both tunnels are 35 feet in diameter, have a capacity of 95,000 cubic feet per second, and have a maximum velocity of 110 feet per second. (Above, courtesy of JD; left, courtesy of CDWR.)

On October 25, 1963, California Department of Water Resources director William E. Warne (left) and Gov. Edmund G. Brown visited the Oroville Dam construction site to see progress on the project. On the right, J. Rodney Mims, project manager of Oro Dam Constructors, briefs them on current developments. Oro Dam Constructors was a joint venture of eight East Coast companies. (Courtesy of CDWR.)

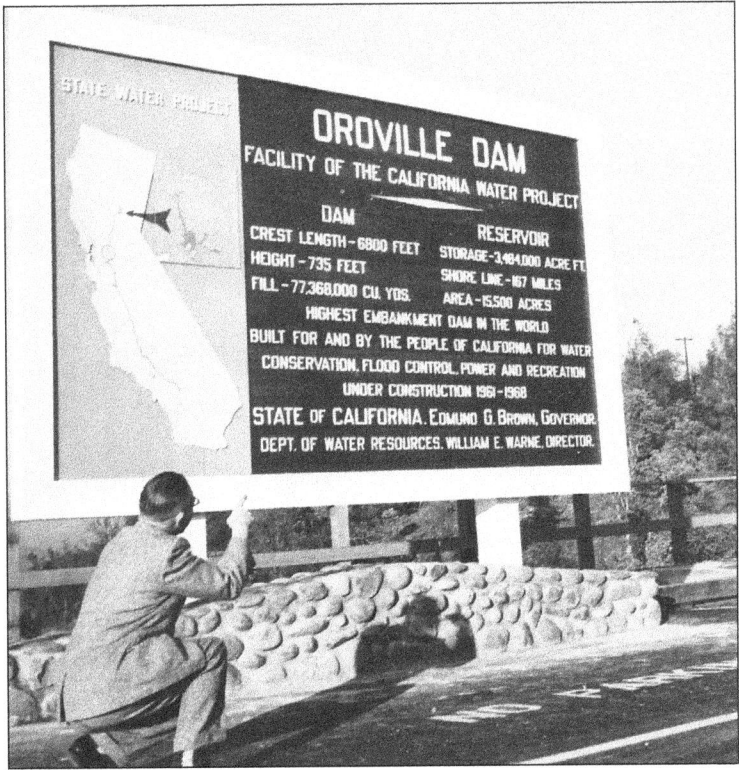

Gov. Edmund G. Brown points to the new Oroville Dam billboard located at the lower visitors' center. In the two years since he had set off the first dynamite blast on October 12, 1961, the core block was well on its way to completion and the Oro Dam Railway had been put into operation. (Courtesy of BCHS.)

Exploring an ODC fill train engine are, from left to right, Chico attorney John Merlo, Chico State College professor Don Jenkins, and US congressman Harold T. "Bizz" Johnson. Congressman Johnson served in Congress from 1958 to 1981. Years later, a section of Highway 65 between Roseville and Lincoln was designated as the Harold T. "Bizz" Johnson Expressway. (Courtesy of BCHS.)

This view looks west and shows what progress has been made on the dam's core block as of October 1963. (Courtesy of BCHS.)

Engine No. 8010 is seen here in good times in late 1963. It is at the borrow area taking on material. No. 8010 was an unlucky engine. It was involved in a fatal accident at the borrow on April 9, 1964, when it collided with a Cat 660 scraper. It also was totally destroyed in the train tunnel collision on October 7, 1965, when four crewmen were killed. (Courtesy of BCHS.)

This photograph from January 30, 1964, shows ongoing work on the core block. The next winter, the massive concrete plug served as a retention block for the embankment. It allowed floods to pass by without the dam losing any yardage, and it provided a solid foundation for the deepest part of the dam. (Courtesy of CDWR.)

This March 1964 photograph of the dam site, looking west, shows Table Mountain and Monte de Oro. Hansell's Bridge sits at the location of the present-day powerhouse at the bottom of the front of the dam. The very first overlook building can be seen to the left of the bridge. (Courtesy of CDWR.)

This 1964 view of the original visitors' center building at the lower overlook shows guests viewing the core block of Oroville Dam. A few years later, the visitors' center was moved to a second—and higher—location as the dam had risen hundreds of feet. (Courtesy of JD.)

Here is the view from the original visitors' center in 1964. Thousands of visitors stood here and observed the construction. Many spent their quarters and used the telescopes that were provided for a close-up view. The core block, conveyer, and truck-loading station can be seen in the background. (Courtesy of BCHS.)

An Athey wagon was loaded with 97.5 tons of earthfill and was shortly on its way to spread it across the dam. The truck-loading station had four air-operated, quick-open gates and was able to load two Athey wagons at the same time. The loading station was a portable hopper with a 1,000-ton capacity. This photograph was taken on March 6, 1964. (Courtesy of CDWR.)

Another view of the truck-loading station shows an Athey wagon heading under the station with another Athey wagon in position and receiving a fill. Other Athey wagons are seen spreading the material, while a bulldozer heads down the hill to the top of the dam. (Courtesy of JD.)

This is one of the fatal accidents that occurred during the building of Oroville Dam and its many related projects. On April 9, 1964, Oroville Dam Constructors Engine No. 8010 crashed into a Cat 660 scraper at the borrow area when the truck crossed the tracks. (Courtesy of GM.)

This aerial view from May 6, 1964, looks west and shows the train-loading station and the borrow area. The Oro Dam Railway's fill trains entered the train-loading station counterclockwise, were loaded, then headed straight east back toward the river to cross the bridge. They then headed north up the east side of the Feather River toward the dam. (Courtesy of CDWR.)

This aerial view, looking east, shows the Oroville area on May 6, 1964, and its relation to various projects. The Upper Thermalito Bridge is visible, and just upstream is the No. 3 Rail Haul Bridge that crosses just before the now-completed fish hatchery dam. Farther up the river is the Western Pacific Railroad Bridge. The Thermalito Diversion Dam has yet to be built. (Courtesy of CDWR.)

Here is a view showing an empty Oro Dam Railroad fill train heading back from the dam. It is crossing to the north side of the Feather River and will shortly go under the Upper Thermalito Bridge. It can be noted that the fish hatchery dam is complete and there are signs that the fish hatchery itself is starting to be built. This photograph was taken on May 6, 1964. (Courtesy of CDWR.)

This photograph from May 6, 1964, shows the borrow area located just southwest of Oroville. When compared to the view that appears on page 10, it is clear that by this date, the borrow area has been well worked over by the bucket-wheel excavators and draglines. (Courtesy of CDWR.)

Here are two similar aerial photographs taken on May 6, 1964. The views look east. Above, the big scar on the mountain is the dam site. The square, white building in the bottom right is Mattley's Market—later Mosely & Shields Market and now Jerry's Market—located at the corner of Oro Dam Boulevard and Bridge Street. Following Oro Dam Boulevard up the photograph leads to the newly built Keg Room Pizza Parlor. Farther up is Stanford Avenue School to the right of Oro Dam Boulevard. At right is a somewhat closer view of the dam site. The intersection of Oro Dam Boulevard and Orange Avenue can also be seen. Just to the west, on Orange Avenue, can be seen the Oro Drive In and the Feather Mart Market. (Both, courtesy of CDWR.)

In these views from the spring of 1964, a new bridge looks down on one of old. The very first pillars have been constructed for the new Bidwell Bar Bridge (Middle Fork Bridge). Above, the Curry-Bidwell Bar Recreation Area with its 1856 Bidwell Bar suspension bridge can be seen. Below, a closer view shows that the new bridge construction has progressed somewhat, and the original Bidwell Bar Bridge location is shown in a circle. The old Bidwell Bar Bridge was removed later that year, saving it from a major flood at Christmastime 1964. (Above, courtesy of CDWR; below, courtesy of BCHS.)

This close-up view of the completed fish hatchery dam was taken on May 8, 1964. The cost of the fish hatchery dam and fish hatchery was $1,096,725. The dam is 30 feet high and 600 feet long. The purpose of the hatchery is to compensate for several miles of salmon- and steelhead trout–spawning areas that were lost due to the building of Oroville Dam. (Courtesy of CDWR.)

This May 22, 1964 photograph shows the Wellman car dumper in action. As the trains arrived at the dam site and were properly spotted, the car dumper unloaded two cars at a time without uncoupling them. It could dump 45 cars, or 10,000, tons per hour. Therefore, it took less than an hour to unload a 40-car train. (Courtesy of CDWR.)

By July 24, 1964, it was time to build the Thermalito Diversion Dam. These workmen are placing DuPont high explosives in holes on the north abutment of the dam site. This dam is located between the fish hatchery dam and the Western Pacific Railroad Bridge. The diversion dam directs water down the diversion canal to the Thermalito Forebay. (Courtesy of CDWR.)

This view from September 30, 1964, shows the rough terrain at the dam site on the south side of the Feather River. The core block and dam can be seen. An Athey wagon is at work on the top of the dam. (Courtesy of BCHS.)

A 110-ton–load Athey wagon begins its journey to spread its fill material on the dam after having visited the loading station in this October 28, 1964, photograph. After the material was discharged, it was spread by rubber-tired bulldozers. Then, the material was compacted by 110-ton pneumatic compactors. (Courtesy of CDWR.)

As the conveyor system brings material from the car-dumping station across the river to the dam site sorting area, the rail-mounted Wellman stacker feeds a storage pile 1,400 feet long. The stacker was equipped with a 79-foot-long boom conveyor. Material was then divided into sand, pervious materials, and impervious materials. This image dates to October 28, 1964. (Courtesy of BCHS.)

This view from October 29, 1964, is taken looking west and shows Engine No. 8010 at the car dumper at the dam site. These engines were General Electric U25Cs. They were six-axle units, and each generated 2,500 horsepower. The first three engines, Nos. 8010 to 8012, were delivered to Oroville on September 18, 1963. That was less than two weeks prior to the beginning of railroad operations. (Courtesy of CDWR.)

Here is a close-up view of the Wellman car dumper at the dam site. The photograph was taken in 1964 and looks west. Since the dam's completion, all of the Oro Dam Railway system has been removed, and this section of the Feather River is now a recreational trail. The Brad Freeman Trail makes it possible to hike or bike from west of Oroville to the dam itself. (Courtesy of JD.)

Here is a close-up photograph of Hansell's Bridge and Diversion Tunnel No. 1 on October 28, 1964. In the background, it can be seen that Oroville Dam had grown significantly in height during the prior three years. It still had several hundred feet to go to reach its required 770 feet. (Courtesy of CDWR.)

This photograph was taken from Oroville Dam's left abutment on October 28, 1964, and shows the work in progress. The routine goes on: the conveyer transports the material from the car-dumping station to the truck-loading station. The material is then dumped into Athey wagons to be spread across the dam. It was a well-oiled machine. (Courtesy of CDWR.)

This view of the dam site shows an emptied Oro Dam Railway fill train leaving the dam site to return to the borrow area on October 28, 1964. In the middle of the dam site, Hansell's Bridge still stands—but not for much longer. By the next spring, its usefulness came to an end. (Courtesy of CDWR.)

Two construction workers ride the crane hook in this 1964 photograph. It was a unique way of getting around the dam site. The camera looks west toward Hansell's Bridge and the concrete cooling towers. (Courtesy of BCHS.)

These photographs show the conveyer system in the borrow area. The 42-inch-wide conveyer transported material to the train-loading station. The photograph at right, from March 10, 1964, shows two employees inspecting the conveyer system for any damage or needed corrective maintenance. In the background of the photograph below can be seen a full Oro Dam Railway fill train on its way east to cross the No. 1 Rail Haul Bridge. This image dates to October 28, 1964. The conveyer system ran six days per week from October 1963 until the last train was filled on October 5, 1967. (Right, courtesy of BCHS; below, courtesy of CDWR.)

Engine No. 8015 leaves the car loader at the borrow area. The train pulled 40 cars, each solid-bottom gondola had a capacity of 110 tons. The operating cycle managed to assure that an empty train would be available on each arrival of the locomotives at the car dumper. This photograph was taken on October 28, 1964. (Courtesy of JD.)

Engine No. 8015 leaves the borrow area to begin its 12-mile trip to the dam site on October 28, 1964. It has just crossed No. 1 Rail Haul Bridge and is making the big turn north along the east side of the Feather River. The speed of loaded trains was limited to 35 miles per hour, and empty trains were limited to 40 miles per hour. (Courtesy of CDWR.)

A full Oro Dam Constructor train crosses the Feather River on the No. 2 Rail Haul Bridge near the Highway 70 freeway overpass. The U25C engines had an interesting color scheme: dark green with a gold stripe on the hood and frame. They had Oroville Dam Constructor's name on the front along with a California golden bear in a white circle. A smaller version of the insignia appeared in the middle of each side of the engine. The cars were painted silver. (Courtesy of BCHS.)

This is an aerial view of the partially completed Middle Fork Bridge, also known as the new Bidwell Bar Bridge, on October 28, 1964. When completed, the bridge totaled 1,793 feet in length with a deck width of 27.9 feet. Bethlehem Steel Company, which had been making materials for ships and bridges since 1899, produced the steel for this structure. (Courtesy of CDWR.)

These views show the new Bidwell Bar Bridge on October 28, 1964. The image above looks south and shows the west side of the bridge. The image left is looking north. The middle span, all 1,108 feet of it, is still to be constructed. This bridge was built a mile and a half upstream from the original 1856 Bidwell Bar Bridge. (Above, courtesy of BCHS; left, courtesy of CDWR.)

Here is a close-up of the first support columns and tower constructed on the north side of the new Bidwell Bar Bridge in October 1964. It can be noted that safety was a big concern, as the safety nets that hang below will attest. No one was killed during the construction of the Bidwell Bar Bridge. (Courtesy of BCHS.)

This photograph from October 28, 1964, shows construction crews continuing to work on the south end of the new Bidwell Bar Bridge. The completed bridge and the new highway 162 would allow access across the Middle Fork of Lake Oroville to the mountain communities of Brush Creek, Mountain House, Berry Creek, and the Bald Rock areas. (Courtesy of CDWR.)

These two views were taken from the top of the south tower of the new Bidwell Bar Bridge and show the necessity of safety lines during the construction. Considering the possibility of a 50-foot fall just from the top of the tower to the roadbed, safety was a big concern. The photograph above looks west and shows a worker with a view of Bidwell Bar's old concrete bridge in the background. The view below shows workers attached to their safety lines. A fall from the deck of the bridge promised a 600-plus–foot fall before Lake Oroville filled in the canyon. (Courtesy of BCHS.)

At right is a close-up view of Diversion Tunnel No. 2's unfinished outlet. The quantity of excavation for Tunnel No. 2 was 220,400 cubic yards. The tunnels diverted the Feather River around the construction site. The photograph below shows both tunnels. The lower visitors' overlook can be seen at the top of the hill on the right. The tunnels were later used for tail races for the Hyatt Powerhouse that would be built in the mountain on the right. The photographs were taken in October 1964. (Right, courtesy of CDWR; below courtesy of JD.)

Both of these photographs are of the gigantic bucket-wheel excavator that worked the majority of the borrow area. It weighed in at almost 700 tons and moved material at an average rate of 5,700 tons per hour. Its maximum production capacity was 6,800 tons per hour. The bucket wheel moved the rock to a transfer conveyor. The image above was taken in October 1964. The photograph below of what was called "the Green Machine" shows the transfer conveyer just behind the bucket. Farther back is the train-loading station. The bucket-wheel excavator was almost 40 feet tall from its tracks to the light on the top. (Above, courtesy BCHS; below, courtesy of JD.)

Marvin McTigue is shown here with his sisters Machele and Denise. He states that his father had managed to get them a VIP tour of the dam while it was being built and that the highlight was getting to see the "monster" digging wheel. The Wellman-Lauchammer bucket-wheel excavator weighed 688 tons. Marvin and his sisters were also allowed to go down to the diversion tunnel at the base of the dam and walk through. (Courtesy of Marvin McTigue.)

In places in the borrow area that were difficult to reach by the bucket-wheel excavator, cranes used draglines to clear off areas of 11 cubic yards at a time. Huge Caterpillar dump trucks were loaded with 90 tons of earth to be transferred to the train-loading station. (Courtesy of JD.)

This view shows construction workers standing at one of the anchor-point tunnels for the main cables of the new Bidwell Bar Bridge. The main cables were anchored by large metal bolts and concrete foundations deep inside the mountain. The wire cables add great strength to the bridge. This photograph is from October 28, 1964. (Courtesy of CDWR.)

This late 1964 photograph of the Oroville Dam preserves a rather rare and odd view. Because of the road on the top of the dam and the shadows produced by the late-afternoon sun, the dam takes on a rather bizarre "sculptured" look. (Courtesy of BCHS.)

This photograph from December 23, 1964, shows the effects of the 100-year flood that hit the West Coast from December 18, 1964, to January 7, 1965. Looking southwest, one can see damage to the Oro Dam Railway and the partially completed Thermalito Diversion Dam. The fish hatchery dam has been inundated, and Rail Haul Bridge No. 3 has almost been washed away. (Courtesy of CDWR.)

This view from December 23, 1964, shows the partially completed new Bidwell Bar Bridge. At the bottom is the remains of the Curry-Bidwell Bar recreation area. The Christmastime flood of 1964 has inundated the site. Fortunately, the old Bidwell Bar Bridge, tollhouse, and Mother Orange Tree have already been removed. As a result of this flood, Gov. Edmund G. Brown declared 34 counties disaster areas. (Courtesy of CDWR.)

This aerial photograph of the Thermalito Diversion Dam was taken on December 27, 1964, during the Christmastime flood. Damage can be seen to the dam and also to the Oro Dam Railway to the right. The flood has receded somewhat from its height. When completed, the dam would be 133 feet high and 1,200 feet long. (Courtesy of CDWR.)

This view shows the diversion tunnels in action during the flood of December 1964. The dam helped reduce the damage caused by the major storms that came across California. The photograph also shows that Hansell's Bridge is beginning to be buried by the increasingly large dam embankment. (Courtesy of BCHS.)

This photograph shows the area near the new Bidwell Bar Bridge and the Curry-Bidwell Bar recreation area on December 28, 1964. Here, the flood has receded from its height of the week before. The concrete bridge in the right portion of the photograph took the place of the old Bidwell Bar Bridge when it was deemed unsafe for traffic in 1954. (Courtesy of CDWR.)

This photograph of the dam from March 11, 1965, shows the great progress that had been made in the previous four years of construction. However, it would still be two more years before the dam reached its optimum height. It should be noted that much of the trees and foliage have been removed from the anticipated area of the lake. (Courtesy of CDWR.)

The work on Oroville Dam went on 24 hours per day, and these photographs show the surreal aura of the dam site at night. In the view above, Hansell's Bridge and a truck at the diversion tunnel are highlighted. The lights shining on the Feather River give it a smooth, almost fog-like glow. In the view below, the conveyer system with its piles of material and the stacker with its 79-foot-long boom are shown at the dam. The bright lighting gives a very odd, almost liquid, milky glow to the fill material that is being dumped on the dam. (Both, courtesy of BCHS.)

This photograph and illustration show the route of the Oro Dam Railway. In the lower left-hand corner of the photograph is the Rail Haul Bridge No. 2 that crosses to the north shore of the Feather River near the Highway 70 Bridge. The rail line travels under that bridge and heads east before crossing the river again on Rail Haul Bridge No. 3 between the Upper Thermalito Bridge and the Oroville fish hatchery dam. It continues up the east side of the river, through the tunnel at the bend in the river, and on to the Oroville Dam site. (Above, courtesy JD; below, courtesy of GM.)

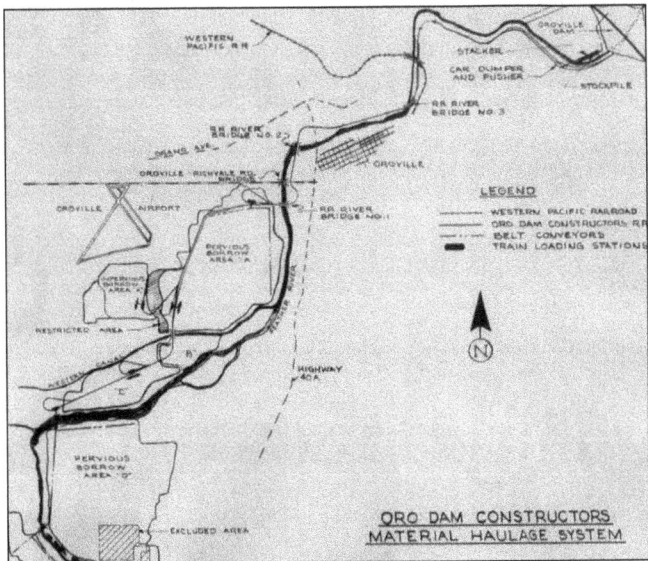

These photographs show work on the Hyatt hydroelectric power plant on March 11, 1965. The power plant, located in the left abutment under Oroville Dam, was blasted out of bedrock. Construction began in 1964, and the power plant was completed in 1967. When finished, the cavern was large enough to contain two football fields. Water from Lake Oroville spins the six generators to produce power. The powerhouse efficiently produces power by a pumped-storage operation wherein water is returned for storage in Lake Oroville during off-peak periods for reuse. Water reaches the generators through penstocks and branch lines. (Above, courtesy of CDWR; below courtesy of JD.)

In April 1965 came the time for Hansell's Bridge to be removed. It had served as a highway bridge for Highway 24 since 1931 and had functioned as an access bridge for the construction of Oroville Dam for almost four years. It was destroyed in three stages. In the first stage, on April 12, 1965, the northern section of the bridge was blown up. On April 16, hundreds showed up at the visitors' overlook to witness the explosion of the main span at 11:30 a.m. One ton of explosives was used. These before-and-after photographs were taken from the upper visitors' center overlook (the lower overlook had been closed for safety concerns). A few days after the main span was destroyed, the southern section was blown up. (Author's photographs.)

This photograph, taken on April 16, 1965, provides a close-up view of the explosion of the main span of Hansell's Bridge. It shows the surviving southern part of the bridge that would be blown up within the next week. While the majority of the public watched the blast from the upper visitors' overlook, some lucky photographers were allowed to take pictures much closer to the explosion. The bridge had been constructed in 1931 and received a design award for being one of the most beautiful concrete spans in the country. This was not the first time Hansell's Bridge had been "blown up." A model of it had been blasted in the 1943 war epic *Salute to the Marines* (it had resembled a bridge that was located in the Philippines). (Courtesy of GM.)

In this March 11, 1965, photograph, construction workers operate a jumbo drilling machine. These units were truck mounted and featured five high-speed drills. Once the holes were drilled, the unit was backed away, and explosive charges were set. These machines were first developed during the 1930s for the construction of the Hoover Dam. This one was used for excavation of the powerhouse and diversion tunnels. (Courtesy of CDWR.)

July 23, 1965, was a big day at the new Bidwell Bar (Middle Fork) Bridge; it was the day that the heavy work on the structure was finished. The south crane tower is being removed. It would be a while before the bridge was open to traffic as there was still roadwork to be done before vehicles could cross on Highway 162. It was called "the bridge to nowhere" until all roads were completed. (Courtesy of CDWR.)

This 1965 photograph of the Thermalito Diversion Dam shows that in spite of the destruction wrought on its progress by the storm of December 1964, construction does continue. The Oroville Dam Constructors fill-train route was between the sidewall of the dam and the earthen hill. (Courtesy of BCHS.)

This aerial view looking south shows the recently completed new Bidwell Bar Bridge on January 23, 1966. Down the hill to the right is Bidwell Bar. Near the upper right corner is the Oroville Dam site. The batch of water south of the bridge is the Miners Ranch Reservoir that was completed in 1962. (Courtesy of CDWR.)

This May 25, 1966, view of the Thermalito Diversion Dam looks toward the northeast. As can be seen, the Thermalito Diversion Canal is not yet complete. The Oro Dam Railway and the Western Pacific Railroad lines can be seen on the other side of the dam. When complete, the reservoir behind this dam would have a capacity of 13,500 acre-feet. (Courtesy of CDWR.)

This view is of the Thermalito Diversion Dam on May 25, 1966, looking toward the southwest. The bridge on the right is the Cherokee Road Bridge that crosses the Thermalito Diversion Canal. As can be seen, that section of canal between the dam and the bridge is not yet complete. When finished, the dam diverted water through the canal to the Thermalito Forebay and Powerhouse. (Courtesy of CDWR.)

Here is a worker monitoring the Wellman tandem train dumper at the dam site. A train pusher used a push arm on a cable that moved two cars forward into position after the prior pair was tilted, dumped, and returned to the upright position. This photograph is from February 16, 1967. (Courtesy of CDWR.)

This view is of a full Oro Dam Railway haul train leaving the car-loading station at the borrow area. It is heading directly east to cross the No. 1 Rail Haul Bridge. The length of track from this location to the dam was 12 miles, and the entire railway totaled 20 miles when sidings were included. This image also dates to February 16, 1967. (Courtesy of CDWR.)

This photograph shows an empty Oro Dam Railway haul train heading back toward the borrow area after dumping its material at the dam. Oro Dam Railway had a total of seven engine units. Three trains ran during three shifts for six days per week. Each train was powered by two engines, and the seventh engine was used as a spare. (Courtesy of BCHS.)

This 114-inch spherical valve at the Hyatt Powerhouse is used to divert water. The powerhouse, a hydroelectric pumping-generating station located deep within the dam, was named after Edward Hyatt, the state engineer from 1927 to 1950 for the California Department of Public Works. This photograph is from February 16, 1967. (Courtesy of CDWR.)

Several Athey wagons maneuver across the dam to dump their loads in this February 16, 1967, view. In the background, a crane can be seen working on the intake trash rack. These stainless steel trash racks serve to keep material from flowing into the dam's intake, thereby protecting the intake openings. (Courtesy of CDWR.)

This photograph looking northwest shows the status of the Oroville Dam on February 16, 1967. Athey wagons, Caterpillar bulldozers, and backhoes continue to spread the impervious material across the dam. The truck-loading station can be seen on the far left. (Courtesy of CDWR.)

In this photograph from February 16, 1967, construction workers can be seen working on the partially completed Hyatt Powerhouse. A 114-inch spherical valve can be seen at the far end. When it was completed and all six generators were on line, the plant could generate a maximum of 819,000 kilowatts of electricity. (Courtesy of CDWR.)

Construction workers appear to be performing a dangerous form of ballet while they construct one of the stainless steel trash racks near Oroville Dam on February 16, 1967. The intake structure for the power plant includes two parallel intake channels—one each for two penstock tunnels. The intake structure has an overflow-type shutter that is 40 square feet and determines the level from which water is withdrawn from Lake Oroville. (Courtesy of CDWR.)

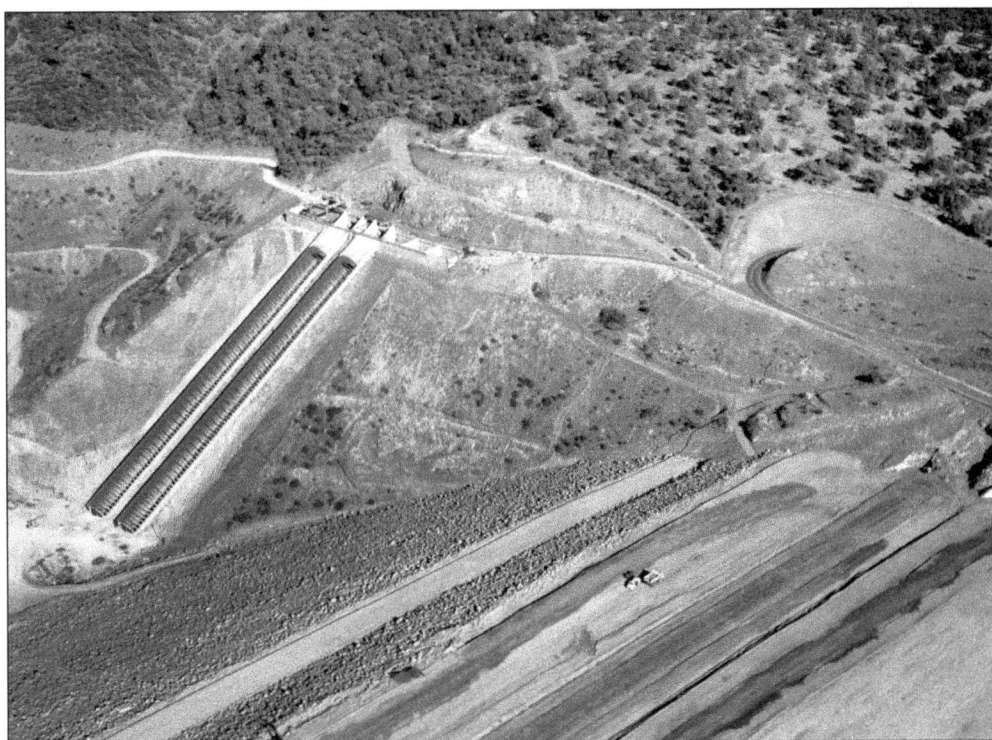

Looking toward the east, this is a photograph of the completed Oroville Dam intake trash racks. The 300-foot-long structures would stay high and dry for the next year or so. Once Lake Oroville was at its full elevation, very little of the structures would show above the waterline. This image is from September 13, 1967. (Courtesy of CDWR.)

This aerial view of Oroville Dam shows it nearing completion on September 13, 1967. When the dam was completed and Lake Oroville was filled, the water spread out under the new Bidwell Bar Bridge, located at the top of the photograph. It reached to the right in an arm up to the point where Miners Ranch Reservoir sits and extended to the left toward the West Branch Bridge. (Courtesy of CDWR.)

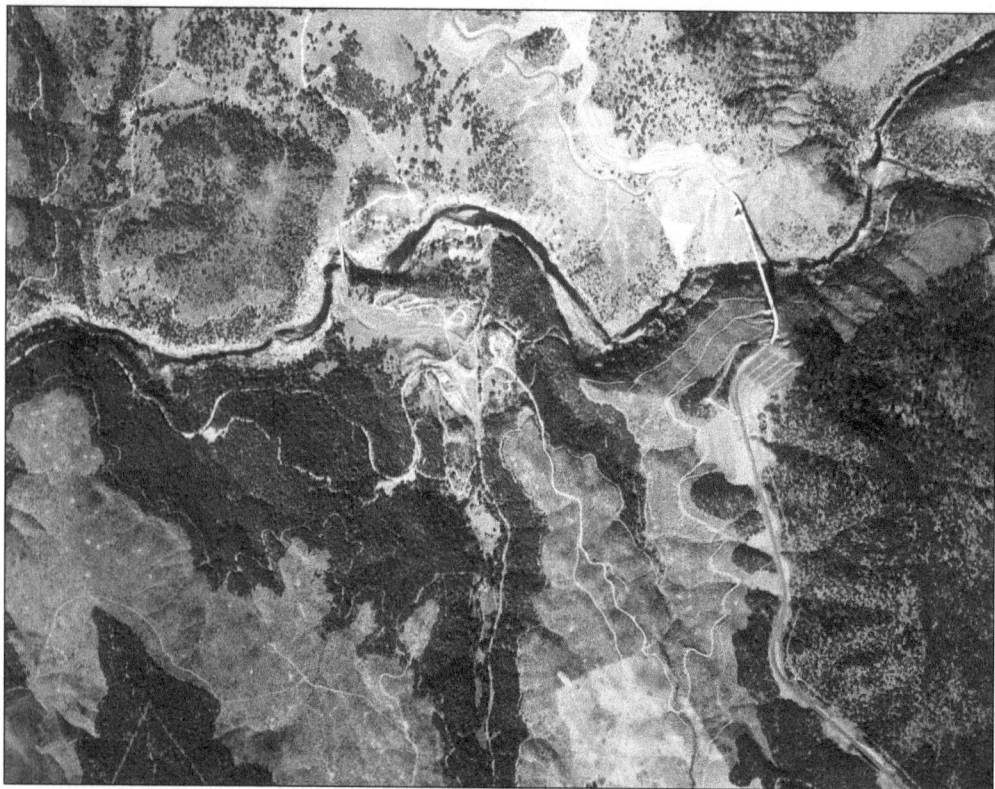

This aerial photograph of Bidwell Canyon and Kelly Ridge looks northeast and was taken on September 13, 1967. The Bidwell Bar Bridge is on the right. Just south of the middle of the photograph is the new location of the old Bidwell Bar Bridge and toll house. A bit farther south is the future location of Bidwell Canyon Marina. (Courtesy of CDWR.)

The completed Oroville Dam is pictured on June 23, 1969, with the spillway in action. From 1961 to 1968, it grew to a height of 770 feet, and it is 6,920 feet long. It is comprised of 77,619,000 cubic yards of material—enough to build a two-lane highway completely around the earth. The capacity of Lake Oroville is 3,537,577 acre-feet. (Courtesy of CDWR.)

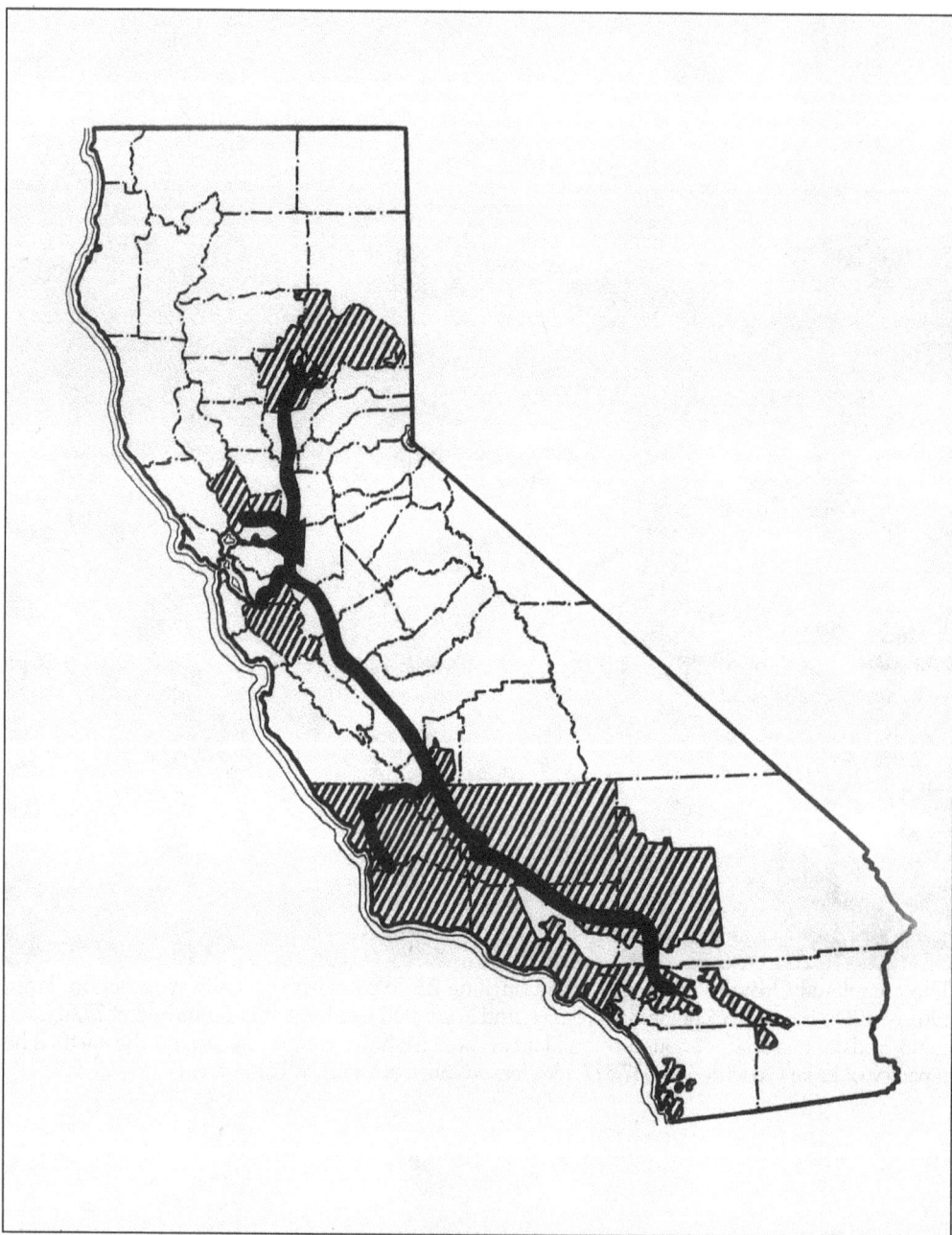

This map shows the extent of the California State Water Project. It begins at the Oroville Dam and flows through the Feather and Sacramento Rivers to the Sacramento Delta. It follows the California Aqueduct through the San Luis Reservoir in Merced. From there, it follows the Aqueduct and is pumped over the Tehachapi Mountains. It terminates at Lake Perris near Moreno Valley in Southern California. The system consists of 20 pumping stations, 130 hydroelectric plants, and more than 100 dams or flood-control structures. The California State Water Project is over 500 miles long and is the world's largest water-transfer system. (Courtesy of BCHS.)

Three

AN ENGINEER'S
BEST FRIEND

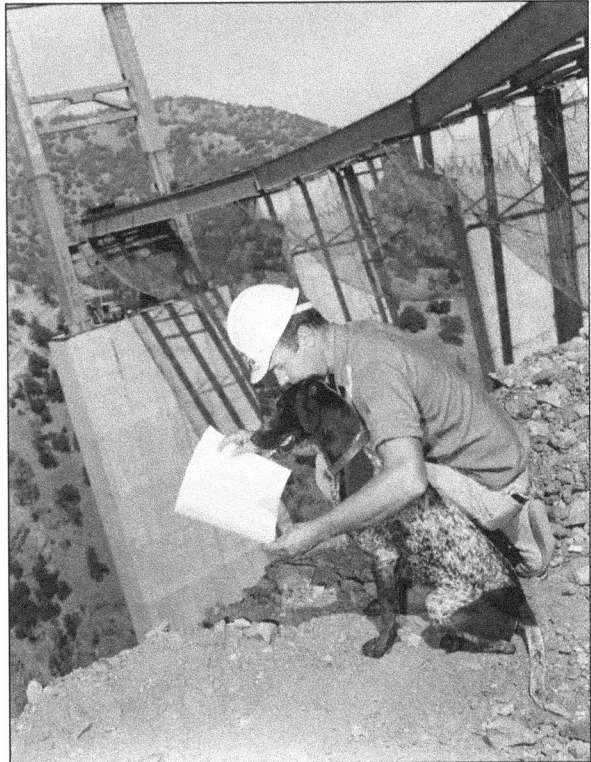

Gene Topper and his dog Moose appear to be going over plans for the new Bidwell Bar Bridge in this September 23, 1964 photograph. Gene was a civil engineer on the bridge, and Moose was his faithful companion for all of his four years on the job. The dog also accompanied Gene during construction of the new Enterprise Bridge (South Fork Bridge). Moose was a German shorthaired pointer and Labrador retriever mix. (Courtesy of CDWR.)

Here, Moose proves that he will follow his friend civil engineer Gene Topper just about anywhere as he climbs ladders up to the main deck and foundation of the new Bidwell Bar Bridge. Gene's family got Moose as an eight-week-old puppy, and his paws were so big that he caused havoc running around and crashing into things like a bull moose (hence the name). But by the time Moose was grown, he had betrayed his name and was as sure-footed as a mountain goat. The photograph left was taken September 23, 1964, and the one below was taken in 1965. (Left, courtesy of CDWR; below, courtesy of GT.)

Gene and Moose were constant companions and a well-known sight during construction of the Bidwell Bar Bridge. Moose was a favorite of Gene's supervisors and coworkers alike. At right, Gene and Moose show their sure-footedness while making their rounds on the bridge on September 23, 1964. Below, Moose seems to be making some sort of announcement. (Courtesy of GT.)

99

This photograph from 1965 shows that both Gene and Moose seem to have had no fear of heights as they climb along the cables of the new Bidwell Bar Bridge. The height of the bridge just from the roadbed to the river was 627 feet. This southward view shows the Middle Fork of the Feather River below. (Courtesy of GT.)

This view is from the top of the north tower, and the completed roadbed indicates that the photograph was taken late in the construction of the Bidwell Bar Bridge in 1965. Both Gene and Moose must have felt quite comfortable at this height as neither wears a safety strap. According to Gene's son Jerry Topper, some of Gene's fellow engineers wished they had Moose's courage in high places. (Courtesy of GT.)

Moose and Gene Topper walk across the almost completed new Bidwell Bar Bridge in 1965. Gene is now retired and lives in Arizona. Jerry Topper says that Moose lived into the 1980s, reaching the ripe old age of 17. During his last two years at Oroville High School, in the summers of 1964 and 1965, Jerry also worked on the Bidwell Bar Bridge as a painter. (Courtesy of GT.)

Four

DISASTER

Engine No. 8010 is lodged in the upper part of the tunnel, having been wedged there by its impact with Engine No. 8016. The head-on collision of these Oro Dam Railway trains was the most spectacular and deadly accident during the building of Oroville Dam. This was the situation that awaited rescuers when they arrived in the evening of October 7, 1965. (Courtesy of CJ.)

The morning sun of October 8, 1965, illuminated the major disaster that had taken place on the Oro Dam Railway at 8:30 the night before. The photograph above, looking southwest, shows the scene from the left side of the top of the train tunnel as recovery workers review the scene. The photograph at left, looking north, shows the view from the right side of Engine No. 8016 and its trailing engine. The specifics of what caused the accident will never be certain; all who would know perished in the collision. What is known is that Engine No. 8010 and its trailing engine were running southward through the tunnel after having unloaded their rock fill at the dam, and Engine No. 8016 and its trailing engine were headed toward the dam with 40 hopper cars filled with 4,400 tons of rock fill. (Above, courtesy of GM; left, courtesy of CJ.)

These photographs were taken from the top of the tunnel on October 9, 1965, and show that railroad cranes and bulldozers had arrived to remove the crash debris. The 40 fill cars that were being towed by Engine No. 8016 and its trailing engine can be seen. State and contractor officials theorized that the locomotives on the southbound train had just cleared the portal of the tunnel when they were rammed head on by the northbound train. The heavily loaded northbound train rammed Engine No. 8010 and its trailing engine and drove it upward and backward into the top of the tunnel. (Right courtesy of BCHS; below courtesy of GM.)

The burned-out Engine No. 8010 towers over recovery crews in this October 9, 1965, photograph. The crushed Engine 8016 is a testament to the violent collision. In the grinding collision between the two, the lead 8010 engine was lifted from its tracks, shearing off the cab of the northbound Engine No. 8016, and was wedged into the arched portal of the tunnel. The impact ignited nearly 10,000 gallons of diesel fuel that produced a huge billow of flame. Each of the diesel units had a capacity of 2,500 gallons of fuel and was kept constantly filled. A pall of smoke hung heavily over the area for most of the night and was visible in the moonlight as a grey cloud from 10 miles away. (Courtesy of GM.)

This October 9, 1965, photograph shows some of the equipment that was brought in to aid the recovery of the wreckage. The view looks north toward the tunnel entrance. Several cranes, a scraper, and trucks can be seen. The wreckage is just around the corner of the hill to the right. (Courtesy of CJ.)

In this photograph from October 9, 1965, several recovery workers can be seen reviewing the situation while standing on the catwalk of the destroyed Engine No. 8016. Engine No. 8010 is sitting atop its flattened cab. The photograph was taken from the left side of the top of the tunnel, looking west. (Courtesy of CJ.)

This photograph, looking east, is from October 9, 1965, and shows a view of the area of Engine No. 8016 that was crushed by Engine No. 8010. Engineer George Boates of Stockton; his oiler, Fred Woolard of Marysville; engineer Joseph Pickney of Paradise; and his oiler, Paul Callahan of Yuba City were killed in this accident. (Courtesy of SOAAHS.)

This view from October 9, 1965, shows recovery workers preparing to use a crane and bulldozer to remove some of the loaded railcars. This photograph was taken looking south, toward Oroville. (Courtesy of CJ.)

This is an aerial photograph of the collision site from October 9, 1965. The view is toward the east and shows airborne Engine No. 8010, Engines No. 8016, its trailing engine, and some of the 40 fill cars of the dam-bound train. This view also gives an idea of the extent of the area that was blackened when the explosion occurred. (Courtesy of GM.)

This image from October 9, 1965, shows recovery workers attempting to repair railroad tracks that were damaged in the collision. Both Engine 8016 and its trailing engine have been moved from their original positions. Recovery and repair work began the morning after the collision. (Courtesy of SOAAHS.)

Here is a view of Engine 8010 as it is being moved from the mouth of the tunnel and lifted from the tracks on October 9, 1965. The cab was so badly mangled that investigators could not determine what position the controls had been in at the time of the crash. (Courtesy of SOAAHS.)

In this October 9, 1965 view, a Western Pacific Railroad crane lifts one of the engines from the mouth of the tunnel. A witness who was interviewed the day after the collision testified that he was traveling down Cherokee Road, located across the Feather River from the tunnel, when he saw flame flash from both ends of the 600-foot-long tunnel. (Courtesy of CJ.)

This view shows workers attempting to repair tracks after all of the damaged engines had been removed from the tunnel area on October 9, 1965. It took six days to put the area and track back in shape, and it was not until October 13 that operations returned to normal. (Courtesy of SOAAHS.)

These two photographs were taken looking south on October 9, 1965, as cranes attempted to lift the engines. Later investigation determined that the collision was caused by the loaded northbound train running the red signal at the end of the siding and not waiting for the southbound empty train that was heading through the tunnel. In January 1966, both Engine Nos. 8010 and 8016 were scrapped at the Thermalito repair shop. They were torn down, and spare parts were saved. Some of the metal was used to build a conveyor belt bridge at the borrow area. The Oro Dam railway ran with only two trains until replacements for both engines could be obtained. (Both, courtesy of CJ.)

This is what remained of Engine No. 8016 as it sat on a siding near the Western Pacific railroad bridge on October 9, 1965. Though both engines 8010 and 8016 were totally destroyed, their trailing engines were reconditioned and back in service by June 1966. The railroad then ran smoothly until they dumped their final cars on October 5, 1967. It took 41,315 round trips to complete the dam. (Courtesy of GM.)

Five

DEDICATION

California governor Ronald Reagan prepares to give the Oroville Dam dedication speech on May 4, 1968. The four people in the middle of the photograph are, from left to right, Governor Reagan, Nancy Reagan, Miss Oroville Joanna Colt and Oroville mayor Conrad Weisker. Also in attendance was Earl Warren, chief justice of the Supreme Court. He had been governor just prior to Goodwin Knight. Former governor Edmund G. Brown did not attend the event. (Courtesy of BCHS.)

On May 4, 1968, Gov. Ronald Reagan and his wife, Nancy Reagan, arrived at the Oroville Dam spillway by helicopter for the dedication ceremony of the Oroville Dam. Ronald Reagan served two terms as California governor, from 1967 to 1975. He also served two terms as president of the United States, from 1981 to 1989. He passed away on June 5, 2004. (Courtesy of CDWR.)

Governor Reagan, in his Oroville Dam dedication speech on May 4, 1968, said, "Here before you is Lake Oroville. Filling to its destiny for the use of flood control, hydroelectric power, irrigation, municipal and domestic purposes and as one of the greatest recreational and fishery lakes in California. And out there is the highest dam in the United States. This is a major achievement of our time. And it's with great pride, therefore, that I simply dedicate Oroville Dam and Lake Oroville to the people of California's future who will benefit from this giant structure and the water that it impounds." (Both, courtesy of CDWR.)

A crowd of 3,500 people gathered on the right shoulder of the dam on May 4, 1968, to hear Gov. Ronald Reagan's dedication. Those attending included celebrities, politicians, and the media. The film crew from KCRA television Channel 3 in Sacramento can be seen.Several members of the crowd are wearing the "Member Oroville Institute of Damology" badge, which was a very popular item throughout the area at the time. Below is an example of the red and white button. (Above, courtesy of CDWR; below courtesy of Scott Roberts.)

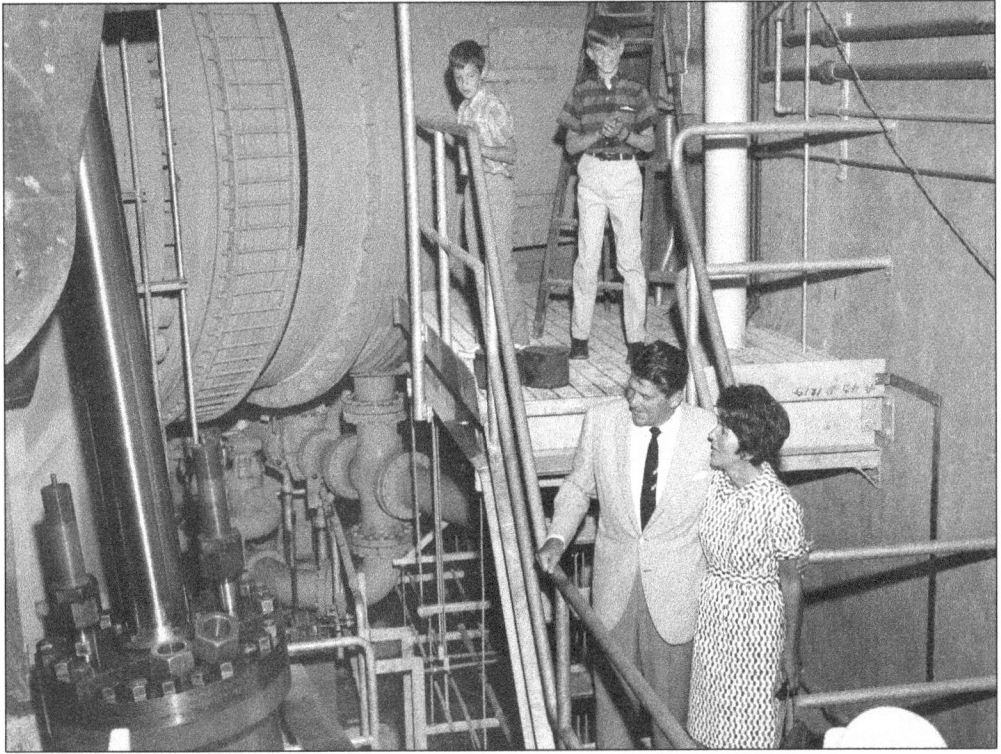

On May 4, 1968, Governor Reagan and Nancy Reagan toured the Hyatt hydroelectric power plant located 670 feet below the crest of the Oroville Dam. The little boy on the left is their nine-year-old son, Ronald Prescott "Ron" Reagan (also known as Ron Reagan Jr.). (Courtesy of CDWR.)

After the formal dedication of the Oroville Dam on May 4, 1968, there was a parade in downtown Oroville that lasted for three hours and was viewed by more than 30,000 people. This photograph is of the Oroville High School band and its director, Ward Pscherer, marching north on Myers Street between Bird and Montgomery Streets. Pscherer was director of the marching band and concert band at Oroville and Las Plumas High Schools for decades. (Courtesy of CDWR.)

A bit of Oroville's past was alive at the Oroville Dam dedication parade on May 4, 1968. The area has a gold-mining past that goes back to 1848. That history was demonstrated by this gentleman and his three mules. The first mule has the name "Big Jack" emblazoned on its pack; it is not clear if that moniker refers to the mule or to the miner. Some folks in the second-floor windows are getting a good view of the festivities. (Courtesy of CDWR.)

Miss Oroville and her entourage were also present in the Oroville Dam dedication parade. Riding in the back are, from left to right, Karen Peterson, Miss Oroville Joanna Colt, and Carol Stapleton. Driving the 1964 Pontiac GTO is Jan George. Burton's Shoes and Gaskins Drug Store are no more; Gold City Mercantile does business at this location now. (Courtesy of CDWR.)

Six

THE AREA TODAY

This photograph shows the original Bidwell Bar Bridge at high water level. It is no longer a suspension bridge but is nicely preserved, with its original tollhouse, near the Bidwell Marina on Lake Oroville. The photograph was taken from Wyk Island, which was named after Waldemar "Wyk" Wiederhoeft, Bidwell Bar's last ranger. (Author's photograph.)

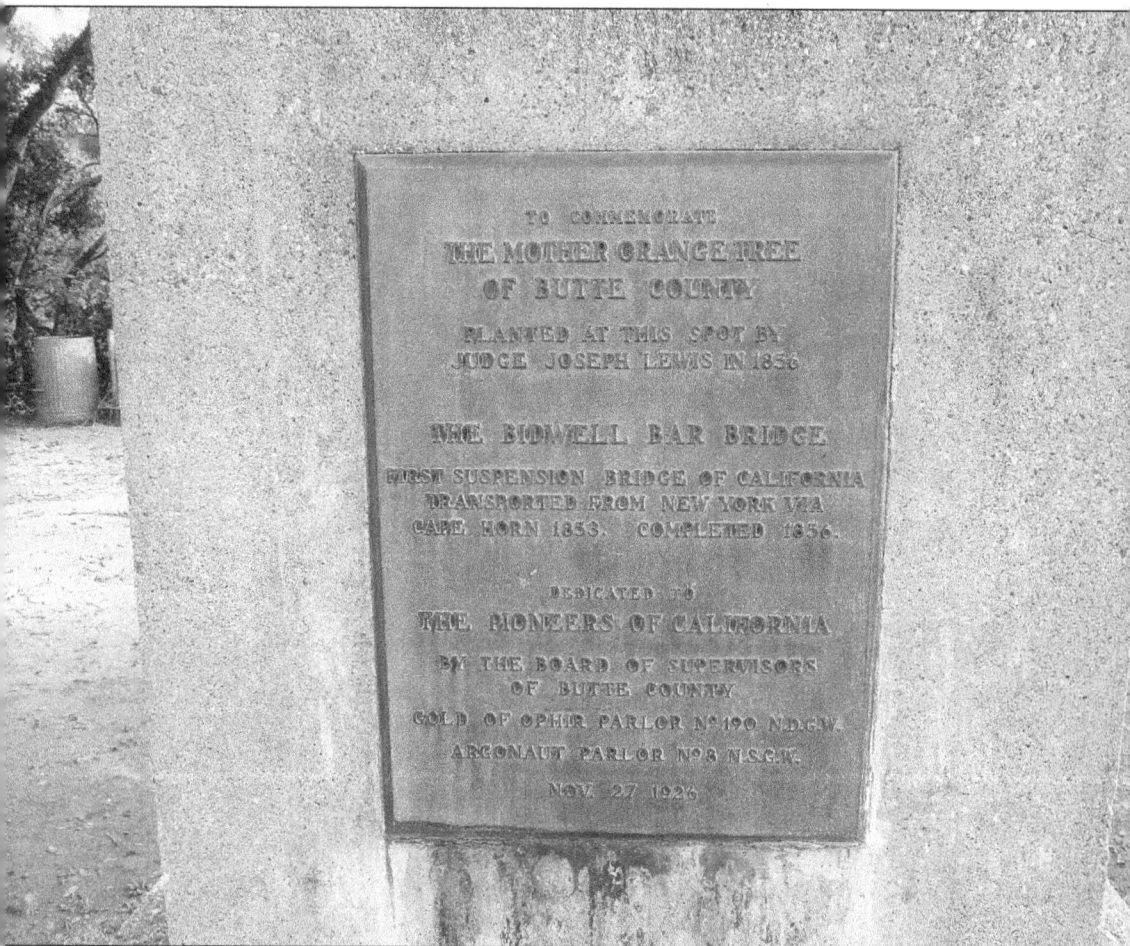

This stone marker was relocated from the original site of the Bidwell Bar Bridge. The inscription reads, "To commemorate the Mother Orange Tree of Butte County. Planted in this spot by Judge Joseph Lewis in 1856. The Bidwell Bar Bridge, first suspension bridge of California. Transported from New York via Cape Horn 1853. Completed 1856." The marker was dedicated November 27, 1926. It, along with several other historic markers, is located near the new site of the old Bidwell Bar Bridge. (Author's photograph.)

The Pioneer Cemetery was established next to the Thompson Flat Cemetery off Cherokee Road. The 350 graves that had to be removed from the proposed Lake Oroville area were placed here. The plaque on the right side of the gate states, "Memorial to those whose burial places in Bidwell Bar Cemetery, Enterprise Cemetery and six family plots were moved to make way for the rising waters of Oroville Reservoir of the State Water Project. May 2, 1965." (Author's photograph.)

The Bidwell Bar Toll House and Bridge were meticulously preserved when relocated to this location in 1966. An original plaque from the centennial of the bridge in 1956 and the rededication plaque from 1977 are imbedded in the wall of the tollhouse. Several other stone markers that were moved from their original location are preserved here. (Author's photograph.)

The Mother Orange Tree was also saved from the rising waters of Lake Oroville. It was bought in Sacramento in 1856 as a two-year-old seedling. It is the oldest living orange tree in California and is now located near the California State Parks headquarters at 400 Glen Drive. It is in a protected area with warming lamps and a mister and continues to thrive. (Author's photograph.)

This photograph of the new Enterprise Bridge, otherwise known as the South Fork Bridge, was taken at lake level in June 2013. After more than four decades, it continues to serve those motorists who choose to cross the lake on Lumpkin Road to access the Feather Falls area. (Author's photograph.)

The Thermalito Diversion Dam is pictured here with Table Mountain in the background. The amount of concrete used to create this dam was 158,000 cubic feet. In 1987, a power plant was added below the left abutment of the dam. The power plant has one generating unit with a capacity of three and three-tenths million volts. (Author's photograph.)

This photograph shows the view out of the century-old train tunnel looking toward the northeast. The beautiful, peaceful sight of water and trees gives no clue that the noisy Oro Dam Railway ever ran through here. There are now lights in the tunnel and a light switch on each end to facilitate hiking and biking on the Brad Freeman Trail. (Courtesy of Scott Roberts.)

IN MEMORY

These men came from far and near to build this great dam across the mighty Feather River. Many a time it has been said, by those working on a project such as this, "If something happens to me on this job, just put my name up there somewhere." Well, that is what we have done, on this spot, to honor these men who died building the Oroville Dam Project, 1957 - 1968.

HARRY K. PHOENIX	CHESTER J. ZUREK
DONALD E. GOOD	ROBERT A. ARNOLD
WALLACE F. READ	J. ETCYL MACKEY
LARRY D. PATTON	HERMAN V. BONHAM
RAYMOND L. NEAL	JOE WEBER
BENJAMIN H. STAMPS, Jr.	FRANK P. ARBUCKLE
DONALD L. McKNIGHT	ORLIN S. CAMPNEY
WALTER R. PADIA	ELMER D. BIDWELL
ROBERT W. PIKE	HAROLD W. CHOLCHER
GEORGE C. BOATES	FRED L. WOOLARD
JOSEPH F. PICKNEY	PAUL J. CALLAHAN
FRANK A. JORDINE, Sr.	EINO ABEL STEPH
LOWELL E. RIGGS	MELVIN J. HUDSON
ANTHONY P. HENGEL	CHARLES AKINS
ALFORD F. HARVEY	ERNEST A. LEITNER
BUEL L. CONLEY	FREDRICK G. DUNKEL
BENNIE BUSH	FRAZER "Slim" HIGGINS

Presented By
Men Who Built Oroville Dam, Department of Water Resources and
Sacramento Valley Construction Unions
May 2001

In a May 2001 ceremony, a bronze marker was placed near the top of the Oroville Dam spillway to memorialize the 34 men who died during the construction of Oroville Dam. Since the terrorist attacks of September 11, 2001, the area has been sealed off from traffic because of security concerns. The only way to visit it is to be dropped off at the barricaded parking lot or to walk across the dam. (Author's photograph.)

The Oroville Dam spillway has, in its decades of operation, been a spectacular addition to the Butte County scene. The polished rocks on the Feather River banks in front of it attest to its great power. During high-water events, the spillway discharge can be seen for many miles, shining like a giant silver ribbon on the hillside. (Author's photograph.)

The 45-year-old Oroville Dam sits astride the Feather River in 2013. The dam is a monument to those thousands of construction workers who came from all over the world in the 1960s. Long after they are all gone, this giant will remain as a memorial to their great work in providing flood control, recreation, and water to California. (Author's photograph.)

Visit us at
arcadiapublishing.com

www.ingramcontent.com/pod-product-compliance
Lightning Source LLC
Chambersburg PA
CBHW080604110426
42813CB00006B/1404